OUT OF CHAOS

A COLLECTION OF POEMS AND SHORT STORIES

OUT OF CHAOS

A Collection of Poems and Short Stories

David Crossan-Bratt

TAKAHE PUBLISHING LTD.

2016

This edition published 2016 by:
Takahe Publishing Ltd.
Registered Office:
77 Earlsdon Street, Coventry CV5 6EL

Copyright © David Crossan-Bratt 2016

ISBN 978-1-908837-05-9

Dedicated to J.M. Hull (1935 to July 2015)

Teacher, mentor, but especially a friend.

And to the memory of John O'Sullivan.

History teacher and someone who believed in me when others had washed their hands and turned away.

Acknowledgements

The author would like to thank:

All those people that kept nagging me to get something published.

All the people that have helped me through my recent infirmity, including the medical staff at Coventry & Warks hospital and my wonderful group of carers.

My inspirational group of friends: Christine, Sue M., Debbie, Rob Nolan & Sue, and Rob & Trish.

Special thanks to my publisher at Takahe Publishing, Steve Hodder, whose patience seemed inexhaustible and suggestions always sensible.

CONTENTS

Poems

Short Stories

"Listen to time breathing.
The breath of eternity is imperceptible."

Edmond Jabès

New Song for an Old Sailor

In these heaving grey mountains of the ocean
A storm tossed sailor thinking only of you
Without concern for life and lacking all emotion
Emptiness only death will see me through

    Let the winds howl and rage
        Let the gale rip away the sails
    Without you I know my age
        Ambition lost and courage fails

You will never understand the hurricane
Or the strange sad stillness in my heart
Waiting for the hurting and the pain
Waiting for the second stormy part

        Chorus

May your future carry you to calmer waters
And rough seas never trouble you again
May soft sweet breezes glide you to your quarters
Remembered love and laughter will remain

So swing the bow-sail across the deck
Scattering the glow of memory and ages
Leaving a battered floating wreck

        Chorus

1

Night Thoughts

Oh my darling one
did you hear the wind last night
dankling and trilling
Before buffeting, blustering and blasting
at the window panes
An anguished stranger seeking shelter
from its own harsh existence
Hoping to blow itself out

I throw my prayers to the wind
Hoping they will carry to you
Across the endless black emptiness
of my soul in this eternal dark night
May you hear this silent shriek -
isolation and terror, as I reach for you.

The Return

Returning to this place
Defeated, tired out, in need of a respite before we
resume

Come to cast off my city habits, my constricting culture
Among the wild winds and hills of dead heather
here to discover my heathen instincts
and to feel the will respond to that savage god
whose only offer of salvation
       is an instinctual scream of existence

Black rock bent by the buffeting winds
Bellows and whistles in the chimneys - Wainstones
a primaeval sculpture issuing defiance across
a modern industrial landscape
       The years I have stood have scared me
       They have changed my shape and marked me
       But no years of change can mar me
       I'll remain when you'll no longer be

Challenge the wind
       I want to be the ever changing unchanging
    whatever is elemental let it stay
    strip all that is inconsequential away

There is little wisdom in words
    books and breath were not at the beginning
at the beginning was blood
dark and free flowing claiming a body to proclaim
    its existence

Dockside and dusk,
    Dockside and dawn
always in the twilight in this area

    Smell of oil on the tide
    Shriek of seagull
    Ships moving lazily down the river

Men with hands like shovels and muscles of raw steel
Strip the bar of beer before lunch
    Tripe and trotters
and still the time to sink some more
    before the 2-till-10

Hard working
    honest day's work for an honest day's pay
    you can trust them anywhere to always
    claim their share
        and who can argue with that
if you're wide enough you win
there is no evolution only existence always
was is and there is no future
do not be fooled by promises

    You pay now or you're not getting it
and she means it straight although she smiles
    There's no credit on these goods
    Take what you can afford, it costs nothing to dream
my dear

Night Ward

Up all night listening
to the bleating and the blathering
of the bedridden

Lord do not let me live
so long that my only friends
are ghosts who visit my dreams

And to whom I speak in a voice
no longer my own but a broken
reed weeping whiney words
to another world with
every exhalation rehearsing extinction in
Seeking Extremeunction, the promise of reunion

But reunion with whom or what
Wouldn't death and dissolution be more desirable
than joining this ship of fools
bound for nowhere each compass point
compromised by the abundance of choice

Dreams of Strange and Fabulous Beasts

Crawling through the undergrowth
of consciousness they come
Dragging with them their sinister ploats.
Fell beasts of evil intent
with drear and dirty designs
where all our thinking stops.

Beyond the resources of rationality
they rise up, ugly faces
which we never wish to see
But deep within us all they lie
Ready to escape
if we give way a degree.

Flight

For the love of clear light
You were a mere dreaming thing
Lost in the dawning air
Clinging to the morning star
Searching for a kingdom of icicles
Scrutinising ponds for their translucence
Trying to capture their ineffable quality
Never realising that it was trapped within
To be appreciated not apprehended
And in being becoming
Enlarged and enchanting but never enclosing

The moon has travelled at my shoulder all night
Silently traversing the outskirts of the stars
And now all I dream is of dawning light
Leaving the celestial angels to their bars
God grant the ending to this flight
Relieve me of these fears

Why I Can't Write a Love Poem for You

A love poem is like an abortion
It destroys the thing it tries to bring into creation
By trapping the truth in a tearing tortured word
Without bringing to birth the breath that expresses
The feelings that I have for you

Solitude I - IV

I

Inside the wood there is another
World in which we lie like lovers
under the seas
While the trees toss waves
aloft and liquid light
bathes our bodies
and all that was world is worthless
in these realms of faerie

II

The belly dancer didn't notice us
trapped in our small circle of cigar smoke
while we waited for the dawn
and for our headaches
neither of us knowing what we owned
as we drank another glass of wine
and avoided each others eyes

Then you told me without warning
You thought we should act our age
and as I watched the creeping dawn in
the dancer smiled and left the stage.

III

The empty sheet lies in accusation
of the past
sitting empty headed in the night
like the single soul asleep in the
honeymoon suite
filled with ideas it can't get right

IV

Alone again in the eternal evening
on a dockside even the ships deserted are silent
searching the snow filled sky for
circling seagulls,
hear them high and shrill and distant;
screech and wheel
as the sun sets below black clouds
bringing ablaze the oily waters

Faustus Explains

When I find it
I will write a poem that contains no words,
That will be a half forgotten consciousness
                of language
lost in a
        subliminal memory
    Nothing of life or
truth must enter these passages

    We must pass beyond life and truth
beyond the circles of existence and relativity
to the deep centre of being
expressed only in silence and shadows.

So She Had Gone

Something happened my friend
Something that we could not control
and that lay beyond our cognisance
when left behind the wire I saw
So many headlights upon the highway
reflections swimming in a different sea

While the soul singer sang the wild
wind came raiding from the north
This is now my only home
Trapped in this ice and frozen air of frost fire
Where time is no longer measured

I do not know where you came from
or to where you returned
In this place it is too difficult to deny
their power or to make demands that they
accept responsibility for so many massacres
implicating us all
The bloated bodies in the dock
stare through eye sockets sucked dry
by grey fish which disappear in the oily current

Do you not know, have you not heard
The cry of the white eagle lost in the mountain mists
She could fly like the wind
across the rain drenched streets my mother
two children clutching at her hands
laughing at the speed she created
and the flames from her feet
Since then I have never been frightened by speed but
I cry at the pain at not being able to fly for

She saw God as a friend
as a release
Not part of someone else's terror
or part of their deceit

She saw the face of God yet lived
and had seen the snarl of axe cuts
modelling two jaguars into a wall in Mexico
saying that she could not understand or care
Then something happened

You Don't Dream

You tell me you don't dream
But your eyes are those of a dreamer
A visionary searching for a meaning
Among all the jumbled lies of life
You are my evening star and my morning star
Bringing with you mysteries and promises

Hard Lines

These are the hardest lines to write
The ones where I want to tell the truth
Yet feel too embarrassed to admit
Like dark matter you fill the void that is my soul
Always unfathomable and impossible to hold
Known only as a sense of missingness
Yet drawing me ever closer
A distance so near but never crossed
But still felt as a desire beyond my control

John the Baptist

The king not being as wise
as his father
Doesn't see which way lies
all his danger
Or from where comes his aid
Or that he should not be afraid
 of me.

Me, sitting in this cell, always second best
While some other charlatan cashes in on my work,
 on the way I have prepared.

All my words, all my message
Come to nowt in the hands of some carpenter.
All my words,
 and all I needed was a word.
One word, that was always away
While I chased, searching
through the deserts and the mountains;
subjecting myself to many sorts of torments and
deprivations for one word that is the answer
to all their questions -
 and mine.

A word of wisdom
 Logos Sophia
 but it never came.

Also, father you fooled me
taking your silence for a sign.
Perhaps the sign was silence, I should have maintained
Silence,

and let the message emerge.

Instead of careering across the countryside,
   animal wild eating bloody locusts
   and only drinking water
   while that magician turned it into wine

  Breath and blood
I never listened to the silence of the blood but only
   the bleating of the breath
with its meaningless whistles and words

  and not prepared to join the chorus
having to be the leader of the band
here I am waiting for a head job.

Perhaps I was using the wrong grammar
But how to construct a grammar for the inexpressible
For all that is meaningful
  becomes meaningless in expression.
I should know, but you wouldn't listen then,
Why listen now to the babbling
  of one preparing for death
     and not knowing what to prepare for.

That fool who thought he saw salvation
through water to wash away the sin
he never had the power to commit
the contemplations little chosen
believing they can take on the sins
of the world with his bunch of
rough necked vipers spreading sedition even
amongst themselves.

The Moon and Flowers

Do not lock your window tonight
Your parents must not hear my approach
For in this land I will steal in like the moon
But still a man of honour
Anxious for the rosebud
And the honeysuckle flower
Yet we must remain a secret as
Your future husband would not like this
As I undress you like a thief
And caress your breasts and body
In a wild tangle of lust and moonbeams
Leaving the flowers on your pillow
And departing in the anonymous dawn
To smile as strangers smile across the street

Despair

As a broken gourd I am
useless and cast aside, worthless
Without substance or purpose
A husk of vacancy waiting
to wither and waste
Lost in an empty eternity

How can this be so heavy
Doomed to the infinity of
a homeless wanderer

There is a Mystery

Woman there is a mystery about you
    that I would not wish to resolve
You puzzle and trouble me and yet
    I yearn to feel the warmth of our bodies
    offering love and life
    and to embrace you in an endless caress while
    tracing the contours of your body with my lips
As we slowly ravish each other's soul
    stripping away the awkwardness of strangers
    with the satisfaction of knowledge
For your beauty overcomes my restraint
    but the winter moon is fading in the frosty dawn
    and the traffic is waking the city
    and soon you will rise and smilingly pull on your dress
    while I silently steal away

I Carried Away My Dream

The moon was already old when
Although I was not honourable you came
We stripped the clothes off each other
stood naked without any sense of shame

Two gypsy lovers in a house near a bridge
A vagabond and a mystic and the other ones who lived

And we turned our bodies on each other in
an ecstasy of lust
each movement taking us ever higher with
each deceiving trust

And as a sad dawn crawled through these curtains
with the city's winter scene
You took away your body as I carried away my dream

You took away your body
and I carried away my dream of roses that would never
die.

Just Words Written in the Dark

Half a box of Belgian chocolates
An empty space in time
No reason to look forward to
the end of work
Two mugs just left to get dusty
Darling, darling girl -
your simple being that made life bearable.

Sacrament

In the mausoleum earth
the cat with velvet claws
buffs against the friendly fist
While Benedictine Kerias caress
the incense night
and Baudelaire blesses the Choir with
- holy water
crimson with sacrificed blood culled
from some forgotten ritual
Minos - be prepared for it is Just Spring and Monsterous
Printemps, les rites
un autre homme, une autre femme
dans le jardin
Digging up bones of lost pets
Shit, shit all is shit and dust
Out of the depths I have cried Credo in unum Deum
                    credo
                    credo
Once more going into the deep how can we acknowledge
And who acknowledges who
shall redeem these bones
So gladly given when no other choice was possible
on this altar built of earth
Mithraic blood flows soft and warm on the head, face,
back and breast
Salt in the mouth and on the tongue
The initiate turns
and returns bearing personal redemption
through endurance of iniquity
Affirming nothing
for all that was is lost and long ago
subject to uncertain memory and faltering faith

Yet sometimes one sees that faraway look in the eye
or the sidelong glance searching shadows
for the eternal moment of innocence and knowledge
of mortality and power.

Joe's Reflections

Joe stood trembling in the corner, terrified,
inoffensive, quiet, a silent shadow in the shadows
Lost in his own gloomy thoughts
His private den recently made snug and comfortable,
warm, dry and draught-free -
Thank the Lord his father had taught him to build
and build well
Had now become a public space full of
strangers, noise, congratulations and celebration.

He was proud and pensive, concerned
for the future and confounded by the possibilities ...
His wife of so few months
How long had he known her, had
he ever known her.

A son, born a foreigner, a stranger
in his father's land
To be nurtured and watch grow
Through these turbulent times of
unrest and sedition.

This unsought trouble, another
mouth to feed, with work hard enough
to find and wages so low
Why had he been chosen, what
had he done wrong
that the Lord should punish him
with a blessing like this,
The thought, half-formed, unspoken and incomplete,
perhaps unconsciously acknowledged and disregarded
He prayed that these celebrations were not
untimely, and would not presage a future of difficulties.

Dock Point Dawning

A delicious tiredness promises to overcome us with
   precious sleep
We have spent this night listening to the sound of boats
   in the port
Watching the lights of the works reflecting on the
   waters and
Dancing in the confluence of river and sea
to the accompanying rattle of the goods wagons rolling
   across the points
And the deep bass hooter of a ship out in the estuary
The sweet smell of oil rising from the river,
mixes with your perfume as I kiss your neck,
Burrowing my face in your shimmering
black hair smelling of lemons, my hands
tracing the contours of your firm flesh
Where in this place and time the innocence of the Ages
contests the mysteries of the night
Now it is pale dawn, cold and creeping in on an east
   wind

Brief Memories

So you heard them crying in the dark
The lost children of Althusa who knew no hope of
    redemption
Cliff top and cave house them and cover
them with mist and
only a child of the dream comes near to
any comprehension
of their fear and pain and loneliness on the
sterile plains of Straxis
Grains of sand streaming to oblivion

For in the luxurious night
The river's dust was soft between the toes and the air
heavy with the scent of orchids
As we settled where purple flags cluttered
the paths
Beside the lulling waters of reverie
Ripples of soft breath against the ear calling
                                        calling
You heard them crying for the small moments snatched
from another's life
While cars and stars sped by in the down lane and
The dying god cursed the eternity that awaited
behind the heavy pain of being that does not dissolve
with the flowers that died in the moment of lies
and evil intention

Yes you heard them calling
                    calling come
                              come
Can you answer come
my lost ones my darling ones

There are daffodils and primroses along the banks
decorated with the stations of the Cross
Mary's Tears on the mantel and open arse
behind the kitchen shelf
Proofs and promises in the pond of time while
words in the wind are lost without a ripple —

See them beckoning beyond the bank
beyond the woods and Far Far across the night
the frail children of Althusa
The amorphous ones forming in the dreamtime to
rise on waves of consciousness and vanish in the
light of perception

Sonnet

It would be so easy to give you up
And get into a routine
You not knowing where I am
No expectation of seeing you again
This easy way of living
At someone else's cost
Grey and fading memories
Of times forever lost
Still I will always remember you
A bright star shining supreme
A source of inspiration
You remain the constant theme
An example of what is right
And a reason to return to life

The Baby

Now the Lord we looked for in the air
Lies lowly in a million mangers
Cared for by a million fears
And granting care on all who care
And solace in a vale of tears
Let every child be a sign
And every one of us incline
To the promise of this birth
For the future of the earth

The Shepherds

Beside the frosted fire trying to gather heat
Thinking of home as the stubborn night's retreat

What is that movement in the air?
A movement as of singing fair
And capable of bringing changes
Across the expectation of the ages

The Magi

The black and distant hills before the clear night sky
The bright and burning stars turn in the morning's eye

Tonight we watch for a sign
For the way the planets incline
And look for subtle changes
In the movement of the Ages

The Middle Ages

Through the blue of Mary's colour
Through the purple of the solemn hour
In the field of cloth of gold
Will the mystery unfold?
And the eternal infant King
Save us when he hears us sing?

So it Happened

Then as you said it would
For all the old time players
who have turned just one more trick
A prile of fives, two queens, two aces
or a run against the rub

I have seen the man with dragon's breath
and the hair of the lion
the one who kills for fun but
that you could not rely on
and now she is only stiff
another piece of cunt cold in
the morning papers and wearing the end of her publicity

Need you every Sunday
Hold your hand, drink a coffee
Flick through the morning papers no
longer bothered about the stories
Knowing they always end in sorrow
The Via Dolorosa is the only way to glory
and isolation the only answer

So I pray for those who care not expecting
any response to my prayer that
day that you kissed me goodnight and betrayed Judas
with a kiss having already slept with him
Someone had dealt the Ace of Spades

So that now in a different bar in another country
I stroke the cat and read a French newspaper
and need your voice but want your body

Having been to Perigueux he
took small interest in woodland
Her body was perfect but he could never find her
and he watched her as she slept and tried
to dream her dreams and anticipate
her expectations but would do
anything just to share a smile

On Margate Sand

Somewhere in the stone desert

Standing dreaming
under an alien sky without even the benefit of clouds

Dreaming of a dead past in a present death
with soldiers sitting astride their machine guns
love rape rut cut and lust
forcing a grenade into her cunt while casting
lots on whether she would explode before
she hit the rocks below

dreaming, dreaming of dust
carried on a howling wind

Sterility of loin and thigh and only occasionally brackish
water
crawling between the banks

No love or justice just another taxi cab with a meter
running

Among the cadavers on the wire the broken body
of withered wheat waits
to be washed away in the deluge

Can you hear distant echoes of thunder in the night
and the eerie sound of ice splitting on distant shores

the growl of primeval battle

Yet we cannot become lovers or even constant fools
just victims broken by circumstance and trying to grasp a
hand

Into the Depths
(out of the depths I have cried)

And to us who had only dabbled with death
it came as a complete surprise
Not in time or place or manner
but in intensity of being
Suddenly the strings were taut
and the lines stretched and breaking
and the blood song in our ears
Nothing now was insignificant or eternal
each moment had meaning and
all meaning was diamond hard as
winter's stars
and every intake of breath was sharp
as ice in the throat
No-one could have told us it would
be like this or
helped us to prepare
For that moment when there was nothing
left
and all words and meanings dissolve
and dissipate in the dense singularity of division

Report on What You Were Not Told

I had not written nor had I lied
about the swords in the sky
Carried by acrobats .....
with phlegm filled lungs ..... dying of consumption
They had no grace .... only
silhouettes of salvation
superimposed on the city shot through with neon
cold as iron in the birth season of storms
Branding their flesh so they should not
forget their beginnings

Oh Virgin Mother
I saw you between the skyline and the sea
giving head to the stranger in
the purple, pink and orange dawn
Trying to keep warm while
they were still dreaming
Where had they hidden the half-born promise
of the future burnt on rocks

Nothing of any importance made sense when structured
A passion play constructed in piss and slime
The actors already bored with the script
prepare to blow the leading lady apart
Knowing the dead can do nothing but rise
Perform the ritual and suffocate experience

How far have you travelled
I had forgotten how cold it is in these hills
Where we shared a blanket against the sleet and sleep
not knowing or caring whether you loved me or not
An unrecorded coupling soon forgot among

the anonymity of corpses
God will give us nothing but grief and confusion
Compounded by the wind in these mountains
There can be no change in this barren earth
our children will eat dirt gleaned from
the ruins that are left us from someone's golden age
We are like smoke drifting and dissolving in the air
incapable of memory or remembrance as we are claimed
by time

Strange Days

It is a well-known fact that cows cannot kneel.
That there is no proper name for the back of the knees.
That there is no telepathy between idiots and bees.
Honey I need. Strange days indeed.
A wife who farts and snores at night
Is better than a catamite.
Clewley's hair aint honey-coloured,
It's beige, it's plum, it's funny coloured.

Madman Screams at Death

It is a cross-handed meeting
On the lull side of the moon
Between the broken dreams
Careering before the winds' wild whip
Waiting for nothing
In this no season of no time
Behind the staring eyes this spirit stripped
This broken body desolate
The occasional flicker in the eye
A sandcrab scurrying for safety
Deeper into the psychological maelstrom
Manifest in motionless physical moment
Call on Cerberus' ship's chandler
To prepare for this voyage
Store away the scorpions of this brain
And pack tightly the salt pork of puberty
Always trying to burst forth
Batten down the hatches lest this
Hedonist isolation breaks out

  In one last try
  Last cry, last try
  To die
     incommunicant

Gaudete

A sword shall pierce through thy own soul

Reprise

"Man, in his dignity, comes home to the unanswerable"
George Steiner

Coming here not as a pilgrim
but as a traveller
escaping from the motorway madness
out of the session of speed
and into the timeless season

Drawn here by a name
and taken back beyond the miles
to a period of promise
What shall we become

We travellers trapped by timetables and diaries
Travellers taking a turn out
Perhaps a wrong turn but a
turn we were meant to make
to bring us back to our beginnings

Where shall we be when the hawthorn
dies and the holly berries await
the first frost of winter and the beaks of blackbirds
Twittering sparrows in the hedgerows sense danger
Will our souls have become rooted
so that whatever our eventual destination
it is always a return

Some things never change
Between the hedges you hear her calling
Where did you leave your coat
Does he know or do you
or do either of you care

Pooh sticks on the river
riding in the flow of time
and the never ending pulse of blood
blood on the snow and in the veins
Christ's blood flowing in the firmament

Across the milky way of memories
and across the grain of the mahogany coffee table
the stain that accuses all of living
the stain of being and to be is to be somewhere
while in the process of being and becoming
in astonishment we find we are arriving
down divers paths to the same goal

The gossamer splits the sunlight into a million jewels
and the rill tumbles an unknown music of stone
ageless and unformed
    Atonal
       Yet behind all this
       the secret harmony of the spheres
Calls — it is here
and you know you have returned

    But can all this be maintained -

The Night and Lies

Tonight I wish you were with me
So we can share this peace
That is only disturbed by your absence

Tonight rain on the river and the
Soft swirls of river grass high
Enough for you to hide from me

Tonight in this distant silence
There's so much to show you
If only we could both trust

The night and each other
But we are avoiding all questions
Of truth, endeavouring just to exist
In a world where meaning
Is invented by our lies

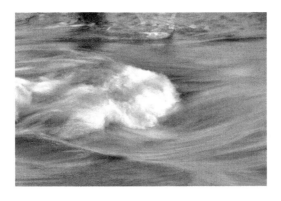

Snatched Moments

For less than a second
Our lives will collide
The endless suspended
The door opened wide

L. Cohen (2006)

These are the times I am alive
When you are close to me
Able to hold you but unable
To push the boundaries of our care
So fragile and sensitive I am scared
Knowing I need to know you more
You offer me compassion I bring you pain

Again waiting in hope that you will come this evening
Two glasses of wine poured but untouched
To be consumed in our communion
Your touch on the door and voice in the hall
Are enough to ignite an undying blaze in me
From smouldering secretly to flaming with
A cold unquenchable intensity

This small time is more important than the rest of my life
To share this moment with you and feel close is such
    comfort
I want to give myself completely to you
Kissing you with a deep eternal understanding, yet
    trembling
In the cold clear heat of ice, pure, hard inseparable
A bond of love unbreakable as I submit my soul to your
    chains
And surrender my will as captive servant to worship you

Snatched moments are eternal and ever present
You are the timeless that is now and forever
You are the emptiness and longing that makes sense of
    life
You are the singularity that makes my life complete
As I collapse into the complexity of your being
Drowning and dissolving in the beauty of your Soul
My nothingness identified and redeemed by the
    simplexity of our love

You have banished time and distance and
All that lies between us are the lies of old lovers
But they cannot come back to break us
As I carry you so close within my very Being
Blended into the perfect unity of nothingness and
    understanding
Marking the meaninglessness of all other consideration
Against the commitment of our love and our creation

Frostbite

Steel, night fierce in winter's claws
Burning and gnawing like rats teeth
gripping with rats jaws
on the bones
Half dead dumbness of defeats
dissolving in drunkenness of pain
burning blue flame
mocking and meaningless at the air's
sharp edge.

Not Quite what I Promised

I cannot write you a poem

Words have only the power to restrict
and how can I tie you with definitions

Flowers are shy before your beauty
acknowledging their limitations

But the wind in the heather calls
that truth I cannot speak and for which

I love only you ....

Old Love

It was only a faded photograph
found long after it had been forgotten
    Covered in dust and cobwebs that it
seemed sacrilegious to destroy
    Now none the wiser sitting in this small
saloon
    Each of us with memories of different
afternoons

    How has he captured the way their
eyes met
    On this faded piece of film

    She had destroyed their universe
Ripped whole worlds apart
    Wrote a new definition of living that
demanded a new art
    Never capable of compromising her heart

    She expected nothing to be given
of those of us who count
    Up the ages of experience as
The sand of time runs out
    While we meander to our salvation
among the moss covered stones
    creeping from oblivion to the ageless
dreams of home

From the Outside Looking Out

Oh frail city
we hear the all night alarum of dogs
warning that the enemy are already within these walls
built of mountain and sea

I have seen your skies
smeared with the sound of a thousand
drummers drumming and your streets running
with bare footed children
Each one carries themself on constant alert
waiting for the cry of
Who should live and who should die
in your steaming heat of exhaust fumes
and smouldering fear
of a smoking gun or "a blade a cut up
yeh face fi trut Im bad"
Loaded with a piece of empowerment
"Donna leave room for reasoning"
under this melting sun

There is nothing we can give and all that is taken is
nothing
The ultimate prize is too big and
Poverty gives power and keeps control in the hands of
the highjacker and their hipsters
With accounts in Caymen and Miami
and an Uptown house protected by security of machine
gun rude boy

We from the outside looking out
at time waiting to explode fear of death and
shrug our shoulders with the rest - just
another nigger down Maxwell Street got
burned by the heat
Someone will have to pay but we are free to fly away

Kingston 1981

Love and Time

There is no time for our love
The moment is now
a sidelong glance, a glint
trapping time, holding us as a glint in the eye
Immortal, unplanned and unexpected
But binding us with steel ropes
with knots we can't untie
Nothing else matters
Time collapses crashing in on itself
Concentrating all past and future
into the eternity of the now outside of time
Where we stand defeated
Knowing that our love set us apart
Free to laugh at infinity

Miles Away

Under 蓮花山 Lian Hua Shan (the lotus flower hill)
I sit listening to the green lake lapping the shoreline
The wind whispers among the peach branches and rustles
the tall grass
Peace and tranquillity surround me yet
All my thoughts are in turmoil with
You thousands of miles away.

The Heart of the Gambler

Your dreams are in dry dock by the river
and the air of the mountains is heavy with thunder
You know you cannot afford to ride the rainbow
or see another bad debt go under

All the crowds that crowned you with laurels
are found wanting in your time of sorrows
and nothing is counted for yesterday
While nobody's counting your tomorrows
You can't get odds on your tomorrows

The dark hand of heaven is turning
but there is nothing left to believe in
While clawing the pillow of the morning
Knowing the cards are so deceiving

Twisted lips and cruel curses among the dross
of the wasted passion that we
share in a casino of forgotten lust
where another hand turns to dust in
a lowly pair waged against the dealer's
final toss

So turning to the window you wait
for the bitter light of morning
knowing that in the light of reason
nothing is transforming the feelings
of a gambler tortured by his treason

Yet knowing a card could solve the problem
and the riddle of the future
for deep in the heart of the gambler
dig the tallons of the vulture

See She is Waiting

In the night's breath, velvet foxglove and honeysuckle
hang on the breeze and a hint of death
and smell of putrification
wafting from the harbour, amid the
Lavantine murmour and distant ululation
She sits waiting just around the corner
at another cafe a hundred years ago, or more now
Crying in the wind, watching the waves
chasing moonbeams across the sea
memories of dead lust
Venus Astarte sweet star of the sea
Sinking into the lost inner sweetness of being
Coming out of nothing, the blank between your thighs
Stella luminary oriental reverie
Tell it not in Gath, publish it not in Ashkelon
Such news is not for the cities of this world
      --- offers of salvation ---
Savouring the hemlock while watching
the philosophers puzzle with their conundrum.
Their's is too great a subtlety
for the glory has departed from the high places
and the ziggurats of Babylon are broken down
returned to desert dust
The mighty are fallen, Daystar son of the Morning
eagle and empire plummet, scavenging with the rats
in the backstreet and the gutter, checking out dustbins
among the clashing of railway trucks
See she is waiting just around the corner
sat at another table with another empty bottle
as the lights go down and she takes another trick
fish heads moved by rats feet along the dock
while the sound of ships moving on the tide
echo across an empty landscape

and the dreams of matelots recall the land
and the eyes of the harlot following the stern light
across the harbour bar and into the empty future
Where she is waiting
at another cafe, another corner, another voyager's end
whether the name is Jonah, Gilgamesh or Ulysses
or simply some other young blaggard
    she is waiting
With another offer, beside the fish quay
near the air terminal and the railway track;
    she is waiting
with sweet sleep and salvation and the memories
of those shaded gardens.

Opening My Eyes to Chagall

There were no storks on the chimney stacks
All you saw were angels and harlequins
playing violins
Where had you withdrawn to in the camps
Did these figments return each morning
With beating wings and tambourines
To waft the smoke of burning flesh
Across the world, their ash to fall on
Everyone's head, their witness of guilt

The voice of the silent forever to sing
Hallelujah, taking up their golden harps
Where the crematoria flames built out
Of the blood, bones and flesh rising
To meet Elijah's fiery chariot
The outpouring of Adonis' bounteous
Love bought in senseless sacrifice

Breaking Point

The black soul that crosses the sun
Can only count itself cursed although
with hands cupped for communion and the commerce
of the damned it prays for forgiveness
in the half light of mourning
At times even the dead cry out
The measure of man is in his forgetting
while not caring to be remembered

> Surely no Coriolanus condemned
> and broken at the point of victory
> could have endured this

but for all that
it is not of a woman's tenderness to
repeal the act
of betrayal or recall the small
expressions of love
The fire of eternal suffering burns slow
and the sin is branded on the soul
of the grateful supplicant

Amon's Illness

Your body is soft and sweet
Your body is like ripening corn waiting for harvesting
Your body is soft and sweet, golden wheat
                    waiting for harvesting

I want to dive into your body
and drown in its depths
losing myself in a region of immortality
Along the sun shaft shall I enter
                    lancing light
penetrating your body with the immortal moment
which is always present, and past and future rolled into
one,
when the harvest is complete.

On the crucifix of your body let me cry out
in an ecstasy or terror where time
                    and the timeless meet,
The Paschal sacrifice; freedom and fraternity
released in the rejection of the old morality
in the agony of the end which is endless
                    and ever new

In the chariot of your body let me ride
Reckless and raving
   lunatic lawlessness which makes all things lawful,
      as the wheels turn. And turn
         again to prove
            that this shout of sublime sickness
               can only carry continuous

                    Silence

Liverpool Poem for You

I'd reap the stars
for you
I'd play guitars
for you
I'd stop going in bars
even for you
I'd give up my schemes
for you
I'd write in reams
for you
I'd forget the team
even for you
I'd raise the dead
for you
Inside my bed
for you
I'll leave the rest unsaid
for you

A Reappraisal

Drifting again in this place
    Defeated, tired out, in need of a respite before we
        resume
    Come to cast off my city habits, my constricting
        culture
    Among the wild winds and hills of dead heather
    here to discover my heathen instincts
    and to feel the will to respond to that savage god
    whose only offer of salvation
        is an instinctual scream of existence

There, black rock bent by the buffeting winds
    Bellows and whistles in the chimneys - Wainstones,
    a primaeval sculpture issuing defiance across
    a modern industrial landscape
            The years I stood may scar me
            May change my shape and mark me
            But no years of change can mar me
            Throughout time I'll stand starkly
            Staring at your strange shrines
            The first nation India
            surveying the wide acres across the moors
            And the Tees valley from
            the grey North Sea to the purple Pennines
            Watching the changing unchanging
Challenge the wind
        I want to be the changing unchanging
    whatever is elemental let it stay
    strip all that is consequential away

There is little wisdom in words
    books and breath were not at the beginning
in the beginning was blood

dark and free flowing claiming a body to
proclaim its existence

Now I see myself again
in this place
Dockside and dust
Dockside and dawn
always in the twilight in this area

Smell of oil on the tide
Shreik of seagull
Ships moving lazily down the river

Men with hands like shovels and muscles of raw steel
Strip the bar of beer before lunch
Tripe and trotters
and still the time to sink some more
before the 2 till 10

Hard working
honest days work for an honest days pay
you can trust them anywhere and always
to always
claim their share
and who can argue with that
if you're wide enough you win
there is no evolution only existence always
was is and there is no future
do not be fooled by promises

You pay now or you're not getting it

and she means it straight although she smiles
There's no credit on these goods

Take what you can afford, it costs nothing to
dream dear

Now I don't miss you, you are not of my blood
These are my ladies
with mouths of steel and minds of iron
and bodies that can crush you softly within their
    thighs
Walking these old streets
Moon rise reminiscing on a quiet
road on the town's edge stopping
in a silence of no traffic
and listening to the town's hum
Watching at the world's edge; waiting
for the conquest of consciousness
to be translated into this town and assumed
into an old communion

But somehow
    It's in all the streets a bold brash confidence that
    buffets you off the pavement
    and swaggers with certainty among buildings that
        challenge the eye
    to dare gaze upon their highs - Babylon
    must have been like this when Nimrod paid his
        navies
    but now it's here and now and always Thursday

For you
    I have made myself hard to you
    and there are no more open questions
    I am learning to ignore your voice and
    You must become less of a friend so that
    I may discover something that excites friendship

Your body has not changed it's just the way you
    wear it
        with a new confidence claiming attention and
           respect
                It was never like this

Apologia

Please remember the promises I never kept
and all the old time obligations I never observed
but do not hold them against me
For my honour was always that of a vagabond
and valid beyond the limit
And love is without honour
An exaggeration of emotion

Do you see now
I was never more in love than at those times
and never less capable of honour

Peace Paraclete

As you read this small twittering
Poem the reality you think it represents will have
already taken wing and flown away before your unseeing eyes

Confronting Mephistopheles

Even now
Reading you in translation
        teaches me nowt
But perhaps there was nowt to know
        or have I simply misunderstood

I watch all your words and try
        to follow their flow
but fall into ragged rhymes that
        rip themselves
                apart

Is that what you wanted
        to teach us

To tear away
        the heart

"Oh lente, lente, currite noctis equi"
Give me more time with words
This confusion can't be true
Still they drag me on and unto
        the black depth -
                Ghennian Grammar
Where there is no meaning
        and no sense
        and all is void and cleft
        apart in this
                dissolution of the body
                        and mind and consequence
                This Sacrificial Hymn I sing
Earth and earths flow
        Time and times grow

Steadily, steadily round the mind
blown
wild
Blood to earth go
Body dissolve so
Sense and nonsense you find
alone
defiled
and so damnation and salvation fuse

The Poet at the Point of Desperation

It is a lonely world inside a poem
   Words whirl and wave
      always out of
            reach
   While you sweat blood
Let me put on my 'antic disposition'

   and run 'Learlike' headlong into the storm
smashed sentences
      blown bricks in the brain

Where ideas and images contend in confusions
      of consciousness
   Which are not of your will
Let me garb myself in the garbled grammar
   of centuries
     half-learned and unable to comprehend
   the age
     or tie it down to the page
     for study by some famous sage
Who will comprehend it all
   and place it in our heritage
Now half dead or not living at all
Among the half forgotten or never known

   And having applied the ink to the paper
in these long scrawling lines
   let them lie there treacherous in the inattentive
attitude

     So he went away again
      leaving with a
       dying
        fall

Distant Divinity

This is the last age, the loss of time
Time trapped between the ages, a lacuna
Where the moon does not rise, no stars show
There is no measure of movement
and we can exist only as witness to emptiness
No longer a face, all personality stripped
and sensation scarrified
There is no centre, all boundaries are dissolved,
ourselves scattered as sand abandoned to solitude
Having lost the ability to adhere,
Connected only by absence, dissolute and purposeless
I hear your song only in the silence and
the nagging memory of something
Lacking conscious expression, drifting in celestial darkness
Deep space, a formless fear, a menacing meaninglessness
Shrieking soundless from the hollow maw of externity

Notes in a Time of Revolution

Curtail the power of persuasion - let
everything depend on blood and effort
No man has any rights or privilege
except those gained through conquest -
be it military or political -
and hold them through might

The light of fools should be extinguished
Those unable to maintain themselves
are worse than slaves and undeserving of pity
Vigilance is the only virtue and a desire
and willingness to act is all that is required
of man

Cold blood and cool logic deny the
honour of man stripping life
of its essential uncertainty and serving only
conservative entropy
Time and space collapse into a singular nothingness
Within the darkness a fire and explosion
of extraordinary power
Randomness and chaos are our only chance
for the future

No longer Ithica or Rome
No longer laws from Babylon or Sinai, let
the demos of the future rely on the epiphany
of power without mercy
Great leaders only forgive those they
emasculate -
for a man better to be dead a thousand times
than to live without the possibility of action
and the thrill of combat

Let the manifestation of leadership be blood

Only those with the strength to kill
have the right to rule
To kill without reason beyond oneself
and to take on the mantle of the Gods
the staff of authority and the rule of
knowing them to be arbitrary

While having the ability to die
without murmur of justice or reward
but to accept the vicissitudes of
faith with a shrug of the shoulders
and a wink into the void
for the tricks that life can play

Humour is also a weapon
to laugh at the meaningless
and those who would be mighty
denys them their power
The camel at the eye of a
needle and the angels on a head
of pin both mock the
possible

The grey dead sea shrieks at
the sky. The bodies of those it
has claimed hang in the
Purgatorial serpentine slurry forgetting even
those it cannot forgive and nothing
returns except a dream

To a Dark Lady
(to J and P)

Oh dark lady of mystery and dreams
Always able to beguile
The innocent with a fluttering eyelid
Or a flattering smile

Not even Oedipus could resist your embrace
And prevent himself falling into double disgrace

Your oracular promise and purpose
Sparkle across the night time sky
Evening star and morning star too difficult to define
Yet we discover that we must try the meaning to rejoice

Within the midnight soul lost and meaningless
A soft spoken voice whispers
And the mischief of dark eyes dances

And inside a life of emptiness
A flame quickens
Bringing light and vision to this open space
Broadening the possibility of purpose
And a promise of a future thickens
Within this vacuous space I hear voices singing
Celebrating with antiphonies
Backed up by the strength of centuries

60

Song

Sailing ships upon the water
    rolling fast and free
All the love you carry daughter
    Laying out to sea

    Take to the roads where
    the wild wind's blowing the clouds so far and fair
    Take to the roads where
    the wild wind's blowing the cobwebs from your
        hair

Time's a mirror of illusion
Smokey blue behind the glass
Stars are turning in confusion
Waiting for night to pass

    Take to the roads where
    the wild wind's blowing the clouds so far and fair
    Take to the roads where
    the wild wind's blowing the cobwebs from your
        hair

Now you're free to ride the ocean
far from the fettered shore
Let us grip this timeless motion
keep us here for evermore

    Take to the roads where
    the wild wind's blowing the clouds so far and fair
    Take to the roads where
    the wild wind's blowing the cobwebs from your
        hair

Bell Rock

(East by North-East falling fast)
Full fathom five -

Charging out of the mighty ocean
The grey sea strikes the grey rock which
defies its advance
on all sides.
Is it sirens or seamews cries?
and the barking of sealions
lends no comfort
along this lonely tower,
in these lonesome climes,
where contentions of seas combine and clash
on this dark outlier
in an echoing silence
where the human voice breaks and fails
Against a symphony of sea and sky
A cloud tossed moon struggles against the wind

Refugee

Was it the sound of waves breaking that woke
you last night, or the pebbles that growled
down the beach,
    Or the chatter of machine guns
that disturbed your sleep with the dull
announcement of death by mortar fire
    Punctuating the air
    Finding that fatal full stop
of broken walls and shattered bones

The feral goat flees the bridesmaid
sure footed even as the earth slips
crashing into the abyss of endless
darkness and reverberating thunder soaked up
in the distance of open sky and mountains.
Is this the only warmth and cover,
Where you're dreaming, there by the water
and cool meadows had you seen
your saint serene in the stained glass
surrounded by the seraphic promises of peace
    Before the air splintered in front of your face.
Waves of power and pain crashing before you.
Dead leaves like other left over remnants
gather round the feet of grey men
dust covered and blown
on the wind of predicated disasters

Getting Out

Amid the concrete and steel there's
no time to be soft
and in a suicide city of neon night
those who aint running are lost in the heat.
Got to keep ahead of the highway before you
bow out deep
Hicki aint trying no tricks
and the pills aint simply for kicks
How can anyone hope to survive and
Living aint just staying alive in this
lonely town
Where the trains tear at the heart
and the engines refusing to start
While the brains blocked with booze and the beast
in the breast of each loser catches the beat
in the dark

Walking the wire with no safety net
The night's on fire and the telephone's wet
Yet the saxophone hammers all the heroes
lost in their own dream
while the piano plays memories
like a flick knife flashing and slashing the face
while those under crashing lights were lost without trace

Got to get back to the blood
Got to get back to the race
gunning the engine and burning rubber taking off
down a deserted road in the dark
Don't know where we're going but it doesn't matter
Got to blow this town tonight
See the stars shoot down the sky

in a gesture that screams at the emptiness
and tells us we're alive
Cos nothing is left for us here just a few
dirty streets
and the soiled sheets of our dead dreams of love

I shall rip out my heart and feed it
to the flames of love for
without you I can be nothing and
emptiness is all you leave

Loneliness lies like a cloud along the horizon

It seems we have nothing left to laugh about
All our days are burnt out and smouldering
Ruins that gave a remnant of a savage nothingness

Tine of the Freeze

We watched the clouds climbing above the dry earth --
as the river bed wrinkled the drought though
The promise of the returning prophet seemed distant
while the children placed pebbles in their mouths
The Makkabah's mystical madness written in the sky
was our only escape from final doubt

and the lady in fake leapord skin asked too many
    questions
never listening to our lies in the machine gun made truth
that ripped all meaning from our lives

Small dogs licking blood from the kerbstones
as she smiles at the stomping foot in the gut
of the dry papped former debutante

A body wasted on a crucifix created from her own conceit
round a mind built on relationships
                contrived to conceal deceit
Gave only a hint of harmony that nobody could want
beside the ice bound river clinging to the frozen banks

Shards of shadows slinking to the poisoned sea
Memories of tomorrow that will never be
Frozen brine on the breakwater
wave lines trapped in ice crystals

all memory is merely the memory of pain and of desire
Tearing lines out of a newspaper that's telling nothing
    new
just further speculation another bad review from some
half baked college boy who never knew the

stark landscape of steel and fire
or the sound of chains rattling in the dark as
the bridge rose from the road for ships
passing up river to unload a cargo long forgotten
from a manifest of greed
While we waited in a warehouse for the dawn of our
    decease
that had already been written long ago

The Fire
of
Divine Love

a short story

THE FIRE OF DIVINE LOVE

*"And there came a fire out from before the Lord, and
consumed upon the altar the burnt offering . . . . which, when
the people saw, they shouted and fell on their faces."*
Leviticus Ch.9 v.24

*"Ths fire blazes in the chosen ones, and makes them (in
mind at least) look heavenward, and to long ceaselessly for death."*
Richard Rolle (The Incendium amoris)

*"If the word of God is not the fire that renews us, other
fires shall devour us."*
Beyers Naudé 1963 (Pro Ventate December 1971)

Thursdays are not a morning for mail. Nobody wants to receive a letter on a Thursday. It is nearly always bad news or a bill if it arrives on Thursday. So to be confronted by a large brown envelope after getting up late and ill after a long night's drinking, was none too pleasant. I picked it off the threadbare carpet in the drab hall of the house I was renting and noted it was heavy. This is usually not a good sign as it means that the envelope either contains the usual unsolicited circular that you wish you had never wasted your time picking up, or that it contains something important which you will have to waste your time attending to.

I carried the envelope through to the shabby kitchen with the vague intention of opening it while I boiled up my breakfast coffee. My eyes ached and my head felt as though it was full of cotton wool and I knew there was little chance of my taking the contents of the envelope seriously, especially as I already resented it for intruding upon those last few blessed moments before you are forced back into the reality of everyday life. Mentally noting that I must stop drinking heavily during the week I tossed the accusing package onto the battered old sideboard that served as a worktop, kitchen table and larder and prepared to ignore it, defending my procrastination with the thought that such a weighty envelope should only be opened when it could receive my full attention.

As I ate my toast however, I found my eyes being drawn again and again to the brown, flat, oblong package. This despite every desire I had of ignoring its presence. At first I did not realise that I was staring at it and when I became aware of the fact I resented that miserable envelope thrusting itself into my consciousness. It seemed to take on a personality of its own and I felt threatened by it. It was like an unanswered telephone ringing out into the night, a challenge that could not be ignored. I could stand it no longer. Whether it was curiosity or guilt I do not know but in the end I snatched up the envelope and ripped it open. I was surprised to find, not bills or glossy pamphlets or the neat typewritten sheets that local councils send out on occasions,instead there was a mass of loose sheets of paper of various sizes and colours, some obviously older than others, but all covered in small, untidy handwriting. They were loosely held together with a couple of large paperclips and as I quickly thumbed through them, trying to get some idea of what this miscellany might be, a small envelope fell free from the collection.

Picking the envelope from the greasy floor I noted the delicate blue tone and exquisite feel of the paper. There was a seal embossed on the top left hand corner of the envelope and my name had been written very neatly on the front in a free-flowing script that I immediately associated with a well-educated woman. I opened this note with a great deal more care than the original and found the following note inside:

Dear Mr Collins,

You no doubt heard of the death of my son last year. It was, of course, a terrible blow at that time but I think I have reconciled myself to it now. Perhaps it was only to be expected that Guilleme would not grow to see grey hairs.

I am writing to you now to send this collection of papers which were found in the room which he held at College. They mean nothing to me but Guilleme seems to have been working on them at the time of his death. A mother is always tempted to keep all of her dead child's possessions, especially a child like Guilleme who, it seems, I never did possess. But he had obviously spent a long time working on these papers. Because they were so important to him, I wondered if it would be possible to ask you, as you and Guilleme were such close friends and you understood him so well, to sort through this collection with the view to publishing a short article in his memory. I hope that this is not too much of an imposition for a mother to ask and naturally there is no rush so I leave it to your discretion. I will not write again but you know where to contact me if you require any assistance.

Yours sincerely,
M. Cecile de Fouchauld.

I turned with new interest to the loosely-bound bundle of papers and carried them through to my study. I re-read the letter and thought how strange it was that Madame de

Fouchauld should choose to send her son's papers to me for we had only met on one occasion while Guilleme and I were at university together. As I remembered the visit it seemed even more strange that the bundle should have been entrusted to me.

Guilleme's mother had arrived unannounced late one afternoon and we had spent an extremely uncomfortable couple of hours playing host to her. Guilleme had been in one of his worst moods, agressive and petulant as though he was angry with his mother for visiting him and this had put the rest of the household on edge.

Naturally I had heard of Guilleme's death the previous year but after the initial shock I cannot say that I was surprised or particularly upset. Strange to say but it had reached the point where nothing Guilleme did surprised people any more. When we had first met at the university he had struck me as intelligent, attractive and extremely rich. It seemed that he lacked for nothing. All his time at university appeared to be spent socialising or at night clubs and race courses, yet he took a first with ease.

Although there was some talk of his entering a career in banking, his family had connections it was whispered, I don't believe he ever gave the prospect a thought. It seemed that he was drifting from one degree to the next and as though an academic career was choosing him even if he was not too concerned about academia. Then suddenly about two years ago, he became strongly interested in the study of ancient and medieval legends and for six months he was rarely seen in his old haunts and his time was all taken up in the library where he was burrowing deeper and deeper in the vaults. Perhaps those years of tireless hedonism had been a necessary apprenticeship for the single-minded struggle in which he was now engaged.

After this six month stint he had set off on a journey around Europe which was going to end with his death in a blazing hotel room in Prague. I've since done my best to discover where his journeys took him and he seems to have been a tireless traveller. It was almost as though he had a mission for he never settled in one place for more than a couple of weeks. There is hardly a library in Central Europe that he had not visited and on several occasions. He obtained permission to go through manuscripts held in the vaults of the Vatican. He was always prepared to travel and would return to any library whenever some clue sent him scurrying back to double check or cross reference. No-one seems to know or is prepared to say how he gained access to these libraries but knowing Guilleme I can well imagine that such a detail presented no problems.

As I turned over the sheets I came across a heavily annotated piece of writing entitled 'The Tale of Friar William'. The title appears to have been given by Guilleme and he had attached an introduction to the piece. As I read it I thought again of my dead friend and wondered if this was the task that had sent him rushing around Europe. If so I hope he found what he sought and in compliance with his mother's wishes I now present it to you, more or less as Guilleme left it. I have chosen not to include all of the introductory notes left by Guilleme which really seem a garbled collection of nonsense, aircraft flight numbers, names of historic buildings and library references. I will let him set the scene and then straight to the story as Guilleme has reconstructed it in the Friar's own words.

Today we do not tell the tales and stories like of old, for the lay tellers and the minstrels are all gone but some stories should never be forgotten. There is one tale that goes back across the centuries and tells a true story of our forbears. It was told down the years as an example of heroism and God's grace and was translated into several languages. But now, like the actions it portrays, the tale has long been forgotten for our Godless age has no time for the past. I have spent many hours searching through libraries and archives to discover the most likely original version of the story which I now put before you. This version was discovered at the Bodleian Library in Oxford and had not been read for centuries but after I had compared it with other extant versions throughout Europe and with what we know of the history of the period, I believe this to be the authentic version of Friar William, that sainted witness to the events described. I have tried to keep my translation as near to the original as possible but I have left it in prose as our language is not designed to accommodate the alliteration so beloved by the author. Needless to say I excuse myself for not being a poet. Unfortunately the first few pages of the manuscript have been mislaid or destroyed through time so let me set the scene for you. The year is 1393 and Duke Arnherm of Eruhurf is at war with one of his vassal cities, Volksberg, because the people have rebelled and are refusing to pay the taxes he is trying to impose. For twelve months the city has been besieged and the people are near to starvation. In the camp outside the walls the soldiers have heard stories of the people eating rats and other vermin. Even cannibalism has been talked of among the citizens. Now the wall has been breached in several places. At this point let us join the story with the soldiers settling down outside the walls before what is expected to be the final assault upon the citadel, the last place of refuge in the city. The attack is due at dawn.

Fires had sprung up around the battlefield as night descended and small groups of men sank down beside them. We had camped within earshot of the moans of the dying instead of withdrawing to our camps because after months of siege the city walls had been breached in today's assault and we were sure of victory in the morning. The men loosened their leather tunics and tried to rest beside the small fires, their swords stuck into the soil in an effort to purge them of the blood they had spilt. Some, war-weary, sank to sleep instantly unable any longer to contemplate or imagine the carnage of battle. For them it was just part of life. Sleep, fight, kill, die, sleep. But others sat and stared blankly into the fire or turned away and let their hollow eyes gaze aimlessly into the night, vainly trying to shut their ears to the ghastly cries of those left to die on the field. And one or two crept, stealthily, into the night to see what pickings could be gleaned among the corpses and to finish off some of the luckier ones among the dying with a quick sweep of a knife across the throat.

It was slightly after midnight when the captain appeared and chose six men to build a stake in front of the city walls near to where they had been breached. It was here that they were going to burn the witch who had dared to suggest that this land should oppose my lord and not pay the taxes which were imposed by him as a sacred right. I believed myself fortunate at that time to be one of those chosen for the work as it gave me the chance to see the city now that the battle was over.

The wall had been broken down in many places and beside each gap lay piles of mutilated bodies. Some were horribly distorted or wrapped around each other by the trampling of successive waves of infantry fighting backwards and forwards over those already dead. Friend and foe were now wrapped together in a ghastly embrace and many stared up at us with empty imploring eyes as we made our way across them towards the city. While the wide gashes of claymores and halbards issued huge red smiles sending shivers into a man's bowels. Just inside the wall the heads of three of their warriors had been set up on stakes and their eyes gouged out. Now the sightless, senseless forms of these once proud fighters made a mockery of all living men.

The battle in the city had been particularly vicious; the fighting had been carried from street to street and house to house. Now each building bore the marks of the slaughter that had occurred. No-one had been spared. The order for 'No quarter' hardly needed to be given for the blood-crazed soldiers had already started to put the inhabitants to the sword. A few had managed to escape into the citadel, the only part of the city not yet captured but they knew what to expect when we brought our siege guns into the city at dawn.

At the time the thought of their fear exhilarated me, sinner that I am, for my delight in their misfortunes. Here we would find the witch who had caused all this bloody affray and dragged so many of us from our homes and our families causing us to miss the harvest in our own land. She would be easy to recognise for we had heard plenty of descriptions of her and her foul doings and every man in the army wanted to see her die slowly for the wrongs she had inflicted. She was said to be aged at least seventy with a stooped back and the face of a demon from hell, all red and pock-marked. No-one had ever seen her feet but I should not have been surprised if they were akin to those of Satan himself for her hands were said to be hard and horny and her clothes were always of the plainest material and too large for her crooked frame. Some said this was so that she could carry the souls of those she had bewitched under her clothes next to her stinking private parts, while others maintained that she wore them so that she could secrete her foul potions about her person while stealing around the city.

Her deeds were known to be of the foulest nature and our bishops had lain all manner of crime against her. She was known to frequently consort with the Devil and his minions and some had even seen her engaging in the most lascivious acts with this plague of hell. It was well known throughout our army that to secure the favours of these incubi she would offer up the blood of Christian children or, worse, first sell them to the Jews for their disgusting sacrifices performed in mockery of our Saviour's Holy Death. We were all fully agreed on the necessity of her death to purge the world of her evil. We were thankful that our Bishops had been able to exorcise her power and looked forward to being the cause of her destruction in honour of God, our Father.

Gingerly we made our way through the city and came to the smithy. There was still a pungent smell of burnt flesh for the forge, which was still glowing, had been the scene of a particularly savage massacre. The smith and his family and many other families from the neighbourhood had been rounded up and killed here. The soldiers had used the implements of the smith's trade for the purpose and had obviously enjoyed the sport because the bodies bore many marks of torture. Some had been beaten with hammers and others burnt on their legs, buttocks and backs before being despatched by a hot poker through their guts or arses. One child, no more than four years old, had been left with a poker sticking through his skull; the scream as his brains burnt was frozen on his face. In the hearth we found the remains of a young girl who had fallen there with a poker in her guts and the coals had eaten away her head and the top of her body.

Throughout the city we came upon fresh incidents of slaughter and soon we came to realise that those who had died in the fighting had been the lucky ones. The well was crammed with bodies. Many had been thrown in while still alive and had died of suffocation and crushing, caused by the weight of those that followed. I had watched this scene myself and shall never forget the wild laughter of the soldiers who poured buckets of boiling water on the heads of those who were struggling to escape. A dog ran across our path trailing behind it an arm, the grisly reminder of how one could be hacked to death and become simply meat for the dogs to fight over.

Having satisfied ourselves that the job had been well done we made our way back to the walls. On our way we became increasingly aware of the amount of animal life that remained in the city. We believed that everything had been eaten by the starving population during the siege. Now dogs, cats, rats, mice and other vermin seemed to be in every corner gnawing at something. They were obviously taking advantage of the carnage we had worked and were quietly devouring the corpses in a matter of fact way. For a moment I felt weak and my stomach churned. Was this why we fought so that the dead could feed the living? But I recovered before anybody noticed and carried on with the patrol.

On the inside of the city wall we discovered a lean-to barn which would provide all the materials we needed for our entertainment in the morning. Quickly we slaughtered the animals, except for a small pony which Gwyther* said he would take home for his son's present. We tore the barn down and chose a strong beam to be the stake. This we firmly planted in the ground so that it would not fall to the side before its task was completed and the witch was burnt. Then we gathered many small pieces of wood and laid a bed around the base of the stake and covered it with a little straw to help the fire catch hold. This is always a tricky part because if you put down too much straw it creates smoke and obscures your view of the proceedings thus hindering everybody's enjoyment of the spectacle. However, Gwyther had now taken charge and he was obviously an expert in these matters, having performed the task many times before. Having prepared the bed, we placed larger timbers around the centre pole, leaving a gap about eight inches wide between them and the stake. This had a dual purpose in that it allowed space for the body of the witch to be placed but also enabled the air to circulate and create a good blaze.

In different versions this name changes. However it is the only personal name in the manuscript and is always a name foreign to the area from which the particular version was collected. Possibly this is to show the presence of mercenaries in the army.

After the fall of the citadel and immediately before the actual event the whole structure would be doused in oil to prevent any unfortunate mishaps or delays. So, satisfied with our preparations, we made our way back to the camp fire and determined to get some sleep before the dawn and the final assault.

At the first grey light of dawn, with the mist rolling off the river and across the meadows veiling the corpses in a grey blanket, I was awakened by Gwyther's pushing me and pointing. "Look! Look!" he was whispering in an urgent and frightened tone and pointing across the field to where we had set up the stake. It was no more than a hundred yards away although it seemed much further during the night. Looking up, I could see a beautiful young girl - perhaps seventeen years old - slowly walking around the structure we had prepared. She appeared to be inspecting it with the detached eye of an expert.

The girl had the innocent, untouched look of youth so hard to find nowadays. Her cheeks were pale with a soft pink blush and her hair hung on her shoulders in golden streams and seemed to radiate light like a halo. Her clothes were simple yet fine. She wore a pale blue dress, the blue of Mary's colour, of some fine material with white lace at the neck and down the bodice and again at the cuffs. Round the shoulders was wrapped a mantilla of some finely worked lace. We were all overcome by her beauty but mystified by her actions or where she could have come from.

She continued with her inspection in the detached way of an expert making a final check of preparations before a great event. By now Gwyther had roused the rest of the men and we all sat transfixed by this vision. Eventually the girl seemed satisfied by her inspection and stepped straight up to the stake. I remember crying out for her to stop and trying to struggle to my feet to run to her. Why I should imagine she was in danger I cannot tell for at that time there were no flames. But Gwyther grabbed me and pulled me down hissing "It's the witch. Let's just watch". Apparently it was widely known that witches with their power to change their appearance often took on the form of young girls to beguile innocent youths. Although Gwyther told me this, he kept a tight hold on my arm.

The young girl - I cannot call her a witch - stood motionless beside the stake as though bound and cried out in a voice of great purity and cold as ice, words which pierced me and left me numb but the meaning of which I could not comprehend. Yet somehow they struck to my soul and their meaning made sense at that moment and, I believe, changed my life though I cannot tell you now what they meant or why they should have affected me so strongly.

As the girl stood there she called out in a voice every man present could hear so there was no mistake:

The priest translated it to mean "If my life has any value it is in its passing and so I dance." But he must have been in error for she stood absolutely still.

Now the whole camp was awake and standing watching her. Then, I do not know how it happened, whether someone threw a brand or whether sparks carried from the camp fires, but a great sheet of flame sprang up all around the stake. At first we thought we heard screaming but it could have been singing. Many people were uncertain afterwards about what they heard or saw but the flames appeared to form a shape like rose petals and gently wrap round the maiden. Her clothes caught aflame and dropped from her body but instead of revealing black and disfigured skin there appeared to be a shower of diamonds and precious stones from her bosom and a smell of roses and wild flowers instead of the usual stink of burning flesh. As we watched, horror-struck, or simply mystified, the flames grew more fierce and became opaque and seemed to dance in a slow spiral of colours, oranges, blues and greens. We all heard a sound that some later described as larks singing and some even say they saw a flight of birds circling round the flames like a crown. A plume of smoke arose and then it was finished. Where the vision had occurred there was nothing. Not even ash remained and the grass was green and fresh as though there had never been a fire.

Around me I was aware that people were moving again but no-one seemed to know what to do. It was as if we were all coming out of a dream and I became conscious of the fact that what I had been watching had taken only a few moments and the sun was just rising over the horizon but the whole incident seemed to be part of another lifetime. There was an emptiness inside me and a longing for something I could not possess. It was as though a parent or a friend had died and left you with still so much to say to each other. But in the emptiness of their absence you cannot remember what needed saying or why it was important. People were shaking themselves and moving away from the scene of the miracle. The battle was forgotten and hardened soldiers simply wandered away from the camp, leaving their arms and tents behind.

Guilleme added this postscript:

A later edition of the story contains a preface allegedly written by the Friar but which is probably an addition by a later writer who was copying the manuscript for the language is crude and uncultured. However it may not be far from the truth for it tells how, after the strange experience at Volksburg, the soldier William, returned to his own land and determined to take Holy Orders. Accordingly he became a monk and settled for a life vastly different to that which he had planned and went on to produce one of the greatest works in our language and, from the numerous translations I have followed, one of the continent's most influential stories. Scholars may argue that it is a psychological classic, or part of the Romance literature, or even a late Martyrology. I no longer care for their split hairs or definitive definitions. All I know is that I wish I had the power to present this tale in its true spirit, freed from the scrutiny of sceptics and unsullied by the scientific concepts that prejudice the mind and language of the age in which I was born. It has long been a delight to me to read my blessed brother's words and I hope my poor translation will give you some satisfaction. I cannot hope to tell you what happened on the field before Volksburg. Naturally I have my thoughts but I must leave you to draw your own conclusions.

We do not know when this postscript was written but it seems fair to conclude that it was during Guilleme's last few days in Prague. If this is so perhaps it gives us some clue to why he should have chosen to bring about his end, if that is what he has done, by the horror of self-immolation. I must question whether this event was the end because the hotel in which he is said to have died was so thoroughly gutted that nothing was left. The funeral pyre was so perfectly prepared that the whole building was destroyed and nothing could be identified among the remains. I sometimes think, and shudder at the thought, that the whole thing might be another little trick Guilleme has played on the world to provide himself with more space. I used to think that meeting Guilleme had been a turning point in my life but it is only now as I ponder upon his death that I realise the changes he is still working within me.

There is a lengthy bibliography to accompany this work which is culled out of the works Guilleme studied and added to by the present editor. In the interests of space it has not been included but the editor is willing to answer any requests for the bibliography and background notes if they are addressed to him through the publisher.

Desmond Collins

I sent the published manuscript to M. de Fouchauld and heard nothing for several weeks until one afternoon I came home from work and lying on the carpet was an envelope I recognised immediately from its quality. I opened it with a strange reverence not knowing what to expect. There was a single sheet of paper with just a few words: "Thank you for your endeavours. As a mother, I feel grateful to you and gratified that my son found his answers".

Signed
Cecile

I took this as a sign of familiarity and friendship. I never heard from her again. Maybe this mystique was part of a family cultus. I am never sure whether I should thank Guilleme for allowing me to be part of this, or curse him for involving me in this family gnosticism.

The Darkness

a short story

THE DARKNESS

Joram stirred and was aware of a slight aching behind his eyes. It was too early to wake; it was still pitch dark. He reached out to switch on the light but found nothing. His hand groped invisibly in the air two feet away from him. In a horrific moment he became conscious that he was not in bed but lying on the floor. At first he thought he must have fallen out of bed but then he realised it wasn't his floor, there was no carpet. He could make out nothing in the darkness in front of him and had no idea where he was. He tried to make sense of his situation but there was no sense. He searched his memory to try and establish how he had arrived in this place but he had no recollection. A man without a past. The thought caused him to grin and he felt the muscles of his face stretch around his mouth. He reached up and touched the soft flesh, his cheeks, an awareness of the bristles on the chin that must be his own. A clue, more than a day's growth, so wherever he was, he had not been there long. What was his past, what was this place of darkness and now the terrifying thought of being lost. There was a cold emptiness. A stomach and the muscles of an anus contracted as though all his being was trying to force itself back to the centre of his body. Muscles contracted throughout the body, without any knowledge of his action Joram took up the foetal position and lay there at first without thinking.

Gradually he brought his mind back to consciousness. He tried again to grasp his past but met the same blank emptiness. If he had no past what about his future, what had his plans been, where had he intended to go, what had he intended to do, but again he found himself thrust into a void. He must have a future, there must be a future, and in an effort to prove it by establishing the existence of the present he looked at his watch, confident that its luminous face would pierce this darkness, nothing. Vaguely aware of where an arm waved in the blackness in front, there was nothing. The past and the future where closed to him and the present was simply a lacuna in which his body found itself trapped. There was a man trapped by emptiness. There were no longer any restrictions of space and time. Apart from the hard wall behind him Joram was drifting in his own universe. He became aware that he wanted to scream and at the same moment was too terrified to do so. A shrill high pitched noise sliced the air and lost itself in the darkness. Joram put his hand to his mouth. When he next awoke he had no idea how long he had slept. The pain behind his eyes had gone but had been replaced by a general stiffness in all the limbs and the neck. He decided to explore his body. In the effort of sitting up he felt the buttocks scrape along the ground. For the first time it occurred to him that he was naked. The realisation didn't surprise him; after all he had been going to bed, hadn't he? He reached down and touched the thighs and calves which must be his own and became aware of the different type of hair. The thin long hair of the inner thigh contrasted with the thicker stronger hair of the legs. Continuing down the baldness of his feet fascinated him. He pushed his fingers between each of the toes in turn. Then ran a hand back up the body to the waist. Fat, definitely paunchy. Must do something about that, take more exercise and drink less.

This isn't how I remember my body, he thought, and immediately was struck by the meaninglessness of his statement. He didn't remember his body at all and if this is what he felt it was the one he owned and with which he must work. His hands continued to run up over his body and reached his head. The beard was now fairly strong and

Joram became aware of what an irritant it was. He started scratching the soft, pulpy flesh under his chin. The short bristles gave a loud scraping noise. This was a friendly reassuring sound and he moved round to the front of the jaw and rubbed gently with his finger and thumb. The sound was flatter and rather furtive. He rubbed harder and dreamed of making sparks and his thoughts brought him back to the gloom of his situation. Now the fingers were in the hair. Fingers twisted it round and round a finger and let it fall loose only to repeat the action with another lock further round his skull. He searched his crown for bald spots, trying to remember what he had looked like or how old he was.

Hands following their own course came to rest on his eyelids, they were closed his eyes were shut. This came as a surprise to Joram, he was awake, but his eyes were shut. He felt again and there was some relief in the darkness. He could understand it now. If only he could open his eyes everything would be alright, there would be light and he would know what it was all about. He realised he must be ill, some strange disease had shut his eyes and placed him in this darkness. His brain raced for any knowledge of any disease that could affect a man in this way but he could not think of any. The loss of memory must be another symptom he supposed. But his watch, he remembered looking for his watch, his eyes must have been open. Were they closed is that why he had not seen it? He felt for the watch on the arm. It was not there. He was now sweating and a cold riverlet of sweat was flowing down his back. He must open his eyes. He must dispel the darkness. He forced his hand back to the eyelids determined to push them open. He was willing to use his last strength on the battle with his eyelids to push away the darkness and re-emerge into the light.

With a sickening consciousness of pain he felt a thumb go into his eye. The eyelids had gone and he felt them flutter above his thumb. Still the blackness. He closed his eyes and tried to cry and heard a soft whimpering sound somewhere in the darkness in front of him. Even his own body seemed to have left him, it was no longer his concern, it was going its own way now.

"I must take control". He heard it but was not aware of what had produced the sound. Take control, control of what, what must take control. In the jumble of words he told himself that it was he, Joram, a man, who must take control and not let the situation control him. He must impress his will on the situation and force his body to obey his commands. He became aware of a hissing noise and felt a warm wetness on a leg. Not this he thought, surely not this, and his mind was filled with revulsion at how far he had sunk. But he sunk or was he coming back, had he always been like this without knowing it? At once these were vital questions but remained meaningless, no answer was possible. In the blackness of his present the past held no illumination, Joram began to even wonder if the body he found himself in was his own or had some freak act of the unconscious mind shipped him into the body of some old cripple whose mind and body had deteriorated to this extent. He was half inclined to believe that and to wait for the mind to slip back into his real state when the idea of an impotent old man engaging in metaphysical speculation about himself appeared too ironical to be accepted.

He was sharply brought back again to the fact that this was the body he had and with which he must attain his salvation. Again he ran the unseen hands over all quarters of his body.

91

Now he forced his body slowly to his feet frightened of bumping his head in the iron blackness. When he stood erect he reached out to either side and his hands came into contact with walls. He turned through 90° and again reaching out into emptiness. A corridor, he reasoned, and backed against one wall. Turning he stretched blind hands as high as he could reach but the wall was perfectly smooth, no cracks or joints, nothing to give any indication that it was coming to an end or a ceiling. Crossing the narrow gap with one hand pushed tentatively in front of him he felt the cold smoothness of the other wall. Desperately both hands windmilled across the wall. A crack was all he needed if a finger could be forced in or enough pressure be exerted to pull his body a little higher until some source of light was reached but there was no crack, the wall was flawless like one huge piece of quarried stone. He searched in his mind for some clue as to where he could be but without success. Words flashed like signs in his brain: prison, mine, quarry, hell, tomb, death, but none of them meant anything. Even the ghastly sequence was empty of meaning. Death empty of meaning but that was death, how could he be alive yet dead? The living dead, zombies. How long since he had last eaten? In the space of no light was there no hunger? He felt again at his body and remembered it was paunchy, he was evidently well fed and he felt soft hands grip a band of paunchy flesh at the waist and twisted it until it hurt. Not dead, the dead are not capable of feeling, all sensitivity is stripped with death. A corpse is cold and incapable of feeling yet this body he stood in was warm and ached where it had been touched. Could this really be said about the dead, how did he know these facts? Perhaps the cold corpse is only the image of a living reality after death and all the talk of reward and retribution was true. But these thoughts left him even more confused. Neither living nor

92

dead, able to respond to sensations but the sole author of any sensation which occurred and unable to decide the way in which to order any sensation in this meaningless corridor. If dead and being punished who or what was punishing him, and what was his crime? Could any retribution be justified, or compensation be made? Then again aware of his situation he was conscious of the fact that he had nothing with which to give compensation, he could not even feel sorrow for a crime that he did not know he had committed. A pang of self-pity entered into the brain of Joram and the cold beneath his buttocks made him aware that he was sitting on the floor again.

After a time another scream tore through the darkness and was heard trying to escape down the corridor until swallowed up by some immeasurable distance. Joram was aware that he had just made a move of self affirmation. The scream had contained the words "I will not put up with this." Again, words flashed in his brain. I will take control, I will know what is required of me, this body was back on its feet and groping along the wall in the direction that the scream had led. On and on, one hand always touching the solid wall he made his way down the blackness. The distance he travelled or the time it took, Joram could not tell; all he knew was he had to follow that wall to some conclusion.

Whether his five senses had become more sensitive in the darkness or a sixth sense had developed, Joram was not sure but he was aware of some change in the area around him. He stopped and listened but there was nothing.

Then he reached across the corridor but the other wall remained of equal distance to him; there was no perceptible change in the light and nothing to appeal to the sense of smell. Nevertheless something in the blackness had changed and Joram knew it. Now a cold fear came upon him, although he had hoped for change this change that was without substance wasn't what was required.

Again he sank to the floor and heard a whimper escape from his lips down the emptiness. He had no will to follow it and put his hand down to the floor to rest. Joram pulled his hand back; his hand had gone straight through the floor, or where the floor should be - it had met emptiness. So this was the change, one more step and he would have crashed down in to possible oblivion. The irony of this made Joram smile for would this be a change in his situation? Sitting on the edge of the void Joram was aware of an idiotic grin upturning the corners of his mouth. He reached up and felt the skin around his mouth hard almost fixed in this idiotic pose. Was this the end of his prison and of his sanity, had this open space reduced him to an intellectual nothingness unable to respond anymore? He forced himself back to conscious action; if there was a gap it must divide something from something he reasoned, and it must have a base. To reach across it, or to climb down into, he reasoned could be the way out.

Joram stretched across as far as he could without losing balance but could touch nothing. Then he reached down with his hands searching for the bottom or for some scrap or ledge to hold on to but still nothing, the void was as blank as the walls of the corridor.

His brain raced, having come this far, defeat was not going to be accepted. Painstakingly he searched the floor all round for something to throw across the gap, or down into

94

the void, something to give him some idea of distance, after all it could well be that he could jump the space. All to no avail, the floor was smooth, hard and clean. No rocks or chippings had been left. There was no way but to lower himself over the edge to see if he could reach the bottom. Fully aware of the inadequacy of his body to accept such a challenge if no floor was reached, Joram eased himself across the edge and gently let his body slide down the smooth surface of the wall. Nothing gave any indication of a base. Joram still had his arms and head above the level of the corridor floor. It was possible to drop another twelve inches, but would he be able to pull himself back after such an effort. Almost without effort he had lost the ability to care, the decision was taken, his body was hanging held only by the fingers. Nothing. He pressed down hard and pushed his knees tight against the wall to help push himself back up. His arms ached almost to snapping point and the veins stood out on his brow, and his fingers felt as though they would break but they dragged his sweating body up until he could rest his elbows on the corridor floor. Quickly he scrambled to safety and found himself smiling again at the irony of that word.

He found himself lying on his stomach on the floor, his arms outstretched searching the wall beneath him. He rolled over again and his arms continued their increasingly meaningless search of the smooth wall. Immediately, an anxious dread came over him and he lay paralysed with fear. But fear of what? The unknown? The unknowable? That perfect clarity that lies behind knowledge and is so pure that man is blinded by it, or, the unknown in the dark that may or may not be there.

Slowly, Joram regained control of his physical body but felt the uncertainty of his position. Inside this corridor, he regarded himself as exposed and out of position. Unable to defend himself against an unknown enemy. Quickly he rolled over until he felt the wall behind his back and strangely safe.

The pain that he had felt in his shoulders and his arms left him no doubt about the body being his, even though it was unseen. He massaged the aching areas and became aware of his penis. If he could urinate he would have some idea of distance from the sound of the splash and this would be much more useful than a stone because you could get a better picture of the geography of the area by varying the direction of the penis. Joram marvelled again at how a man's intellect could provide the tools to overcome the constrictions of any situation. He took up position as close as he dared to the void and tried to force himself to urinate with the greatest pressure he could exert. He felt his penis come alive in his hand and the surge of warm liquid along the urethra and out over the edge of darkness. He directed his penis to the right and then the left and waited for some response out of the darkness. He strained his ears for a reply but there was nothing. The blackness had taken and nothing had been returned. Joram had stopped urinating and tried to comprehend what the silence meant.

Could it be that there was nothing in front of him or below him? Everything that existed must be behind him. He considered retracing his steps, making his way back down that emptiness where there had been no meaning but in which he had sought sense. But what if he did go back, Joram now thought it likely that it would come to an end just as this one did - an open space in which to do what?

Then there was light and Joram could see all that he needed but the corridor remained as dark and anonymous as before. He saw how his body had been trapped and how it had tried to escape. Then the life which he thought he controlled, how it had been walled in on every side, controlled and directed in meaninglessness. His captivity was of his own making and acceptance. The gap was the means of escape, he decided. But did he want to escape and to what would he escape? Would he clear the gap and find the answers that the corridor had brought to his consciousness or was there just the void? The illumination that had first brought joy to Joram now brought with it the terrors of the possibility of certainty.

Joram rose to his feet and backed slowly away from the gap, aware of the heaviness of his body as a solid living whole. The bulk settled back on his heels and he felt himself standing flat-footed and square. Totally independent and in control in this dark universe which he intended to shatter. He felt the strength in his calves and thighs, the spring in his ankles and the driving power of his shoulder and he wondered as he started his run, would they have the power to carry him across? Joram felt the end of the corridor slip away beneath him as he launched himself across the emptiness.

Lightning Source UK Ltd.
Milton Keynes UK
UKOW07n1404181016